PRESENCE: an impressive manner of being where one remains calm, in the current reality and can take quick, sensible actions.

"Until one is committed there is hesitancy, the chance to draw back, always ineffectiveness. Concerning all acts of initiative or creation, there is one elementary truth...that the moment one definitely commits oneself, then Providence moves. too. All sorts of things occur to help one that would otherwise never have occurred. A whole stream of events issues from the decision, raising in one's favor all manner of incidents and meetings and material assistance which no man would have believed would have come his way.

Whatever you think you can do or believe you can do, begin it. Boldness has magic, grace, and power in it."

W. H. Murray in The Scottish Himalayan Expedition

Tilt365.com

Tilt
Presence

Be the calm in a sea of noise

By Pam Boney

Illustration by Bob Ostrom

CONTENTS

1. The Path to a Life Well Lived

2. Kiss Your Wake-Up Call

3. The Unexamined Life Script

4. Rigid vs. Agile Mindset

5. Fight, Flee, Freeze, or deFlect

6. Foe or FOO—Know the Difference

7. Your FOO Is Your Responsibility

8. How FOO Looks on the Surface

9. Can People Really Change?

10. Your Inner Circle

11. The Eight Essential Questions

12. The Path to Rock-Solid Presence

13. Question #1 Am I Safe? (Security vs. Mistrust)

14. Question #2 Am I Capable? (Power vs. Self-Doubt)

15. Question #3 Am I Good? (Approval vs. Rejection)

16. Question #4 Am I Special? (Attention vs. Guilt/Shame)

17. You Are the Final Judge of You

18. Question #5 Am I Important? (Status vs. Insignificance)

19. Question #6 Am I Productive? (Autonomy vs. Dependence)

20. Question #7 Am I Valued? (Acceptance vs. Isolation)

21. Question #8 Am I Worthy? (Recognition vs. Despair)

22. Final Reflection

Be the calm in a sea of noise.

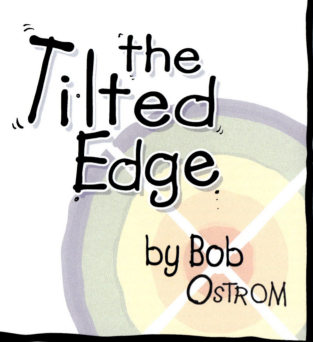

The Path to a Life Well-Lived

All of us want to be able to say we lived a good life and did great things. But most of us are not sure how to accomplish this goal on a day-to-day basis, always asking one simple question: Why am I here? This book is for those of us who want to know more about why we do what we do... and how our actions relate to our outcomes, both personal and professional. It's also for those who not only want to find their creative purpose and meaning for being here but also want to accomplish it.

The book takes a work perspective because, as an executive coach with two decades of experience, I've learned that no matter where we learn important wisdoms, we can usually still apply them to other parts of our life. Your work may be to raise a great family as easily as it may be to run a company, build great software, or launch a social cause. Whatever it is, it is your work to do and you must do it heartily. The purpose of this book is to help you get a clear grasp of what makes you happy—how to filter out the noise and focus on what will ultimately help you feel a deep sense of purpose about your efforts and, in turn, your life and work.

If you are a seeker of self-knowledge and want to live a more intentional version of yourself, you'll find the clues you need here. We become what we most expect to see, because our eyes look for what validates our earliest experiences and beliefs. For example, if we developed a belief that the world is imperfect, our attention will look for what isn't perfect everywhere we go. By repeated experience, we then learn to be skilled at perfecting things. The question is whether this skill brings us joy or feels like a burden. This book helps us to be open and surprised by the greatness that is possible for each of us when we tap into a more purposeful version of ourselves that amps up our inner creative genius.

This book is for those who are stargazers. Those who dream big and embrace the creative spontaneity that is the universe. Those who want to find and complete their creative purpose—the one compulsory directive of a life well lived. Those who know they can't afford to live a life someone else prescribed for them.

I believe it is our highest moral imperative to find and deliver our legacy. Whether it is to raise great children, make our community prettier or cleaner, help people get healthy, solve a complex problem, invent something better, create something new, or start something that lives on beyond us. Whatever it is, we must know it and live it with every waking day and every ounce of our energy until we feel complete. It isn't an easy path. In fact, it's quite challenging and often backbreaking. But the character-building inherent in the challenge is what makes it feel great. Doing something difficult and finishing well is the one thing that drives self-respect and self-acceptance. Happiness, success, money, and all of the external trappings are by-products of finding our service to the world. They are not our purpose, so they will never fill the insatiable hole inside us, nor provide the feeling of moral accomplishment from grappling with a challenge that fulfills our creative purpose. Finding and mastering our gift to the world, small or large, is absolutely everything.

If you know what your purpose is, this book will make it even clearer. If you don't, it will hopefully inspire you to claim your place in the world and find your most powerful voice.

It may also prevent you from living an unexamined script and from living a life that was never really meant to be yours.

My Notes

Kiss Your Wake-Up Call

I used to think my story was unusual. It went a little something like this:

I woke up one day and realized I had created my own self-fulfilling prophecy. I had succeeded professionally, and with the extreme commitment it took to do so, I had succeeded in something else unimaginable and unintended. Somehow, I had managed to ruin my personal life, which was a mess born of neglect and questionable character. Trophy in hand, I walked back to my hotel room and sat on the side of my bed, choking back my tears. I had just won a coveted top award I had wanted for the last five years. And there was no one to call who would care, except my team, and they were asleep in bed by now. The quiet ringing in my ears was deafening. I'd heard that sound as a child and remembered the experience as terrifying. Aloneness. Loss. Emptiness. Then uncertainty about what to do next. Nothing to do. Nothing to distract me. Alone. Deeply sad. Unable to avoid the void I felt inside any longer. There was something missing in there. The trophy felt like an ice-cold mirror of my heart.

As I sat there alone in my room, I recalled the words of a friend who volunteered for a hospice, sitting with people in their last days. She once told me that people die one of two ways. The first group of people were fulfilled and peaceful, gracefully making their exit with gratitude for a life well lived. In that most daunting moment of facing mortality, they seemed to accept with grace—with an air of presence—that their life on earth was coming to an end. They seemed to be resolved on the idea that death is part of life, and the possibility of it was the one thing that made each day matter more. Instead of fearing death, they saw it as a natural motivator for each precious moment. Most importantly, they showed their caregivers how to die with grace and without fear. The ultimate act of courage.

The second group of people departed this world in anger and despair. Some fought to the death, even frightening their caregivers, leaving behind a vivid memory of fear and anguish about their own ultimate mortality. When I first heard this, I had to wonder what the driving force for this stark duality was. Could it be that anger and despair resulted in those who did not take time to examine their life stories—to explore the "why" behind every big motivation and every small moment that made up their lives? Were they living each day to seek more pleasure and avoid more pain but not thinking about where those daily actions would ultimately lead? Did they have a short-sighted, biased world view, where everything was black and white, so they never grew into who they could have been?

That night I could see a huge brick wall towering in front of me. I began to question myself and what I would experience at the end of life. It was then that I remembered a phrase that explained this idea of a life unlived to its fullest extent: the unexamined life script. Where had I read it? Reflecting on the concept, I asked myself, had those in despair lived an unexamined life script, never stopping to question the story by which they conducted their day-to-day life? Thus, they missed the point of the precious resource of life and forgot to live their own. I realized many people live their lives running from the past or striving for the future, unconscious fear driving them to miss the present moment. Miss the implications. This contrast hit close to home for me. I was missing what was most important.

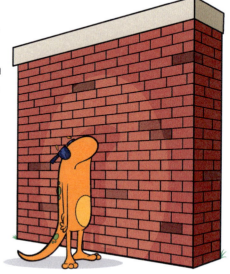

And so it began. That brick wall towered in front of me . . . I knew climbing up over it to the other side would be hard work. But, determined with a new perspective, the next day I walked out of that room and began to change my life in a new way. I stopped striving so much to succeed, to be the best, to win the prize. Instead my changes focused on having more balance; they seemed subtle, but over time they made climbing that brick wall possible. And what did I do to change my life?

I began to examine it. Reflect upon it. Listen to the small, still voice inside me. Listen to what mattered most and what Providence would make of me. I began to seek answers then. And that always starts with questions. Existential ones. And presence in each moment.

REFLECTION:
Make a list of your top 7–10 interests. Where do they come together to make you one of a kind, with a unique blend of interests? Notice that your interests are there for a reason.

8 Questions

1: **Am I safe?** (Security vs. Mistrust)

2: **Am I capable?** (Power vs. Self-Doubt)

3: **Am I good?** (Approval vs. Rejection)

4: **Am I special?** (Attention vs. Guilt/Shame)

5: **Am I important?** (Status vs. Insignificance)

6: **Am I productive?** (Autonomy vs. Dependence)

7: **Am I valued?** (Acceptance vs. Isolation)

8: **Am I worthy?** (Recognition vs. Despair)

To live the good life and contribute our true creative purpose in the world, we must answer eight existential questions that reside in our inner identity. The first four are hopefully answered in our first twenty years of development into an adult, before we embark on our journey into the world as individuals. If not, we can live unaware of these powerful needs inside ourselves and even lose our way. If we are unable to form affirmative answers early on in life, we must face them in our adult lives and grapple with lessons that can teach us how to grow a strong internal identity. And having a strong sense of self is ultimately what helps us find our vocation and contributions to the world. Left unanswered, they will lurk under the surface and drive our behaviors without awareness, yet haunting us with repetitive, self-fulfilling prophecies that follow us everywhere we go. How do we know? Because we keep getting the same frustrating results we don't want. That's where the clues can be found and our identity work can begin in earnest. If your answer to one or more of them is "maybe" or "no", it's never too late to seek answers to these important questions- then open the door to your most creative contribution yet. The important choice is to begin right now for it is never too early or late.

Personality is where we begin, but it's our character that truly shapes our destiny.

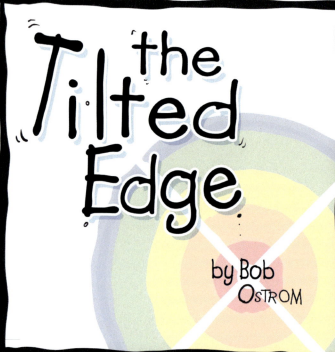

The Unexamined Life-Script

Heartbreaking as my own story was to me, I've learned since that if you stop telling your own stories and start listening to the stories of others, you realize almost everyone has a story that will both warm your heart and astound you with their capacity for human resilience. I've been surprised to learn that often the darkest periods in a person's life can become the catalyst for their ultimate greatness, the starting point for an upward trajectory of change. Why does this happen? In almost every case, that life-defining moment woke them up to an unexamined life script—a script that was lurking underneath and driving more of their life than they realized.

The script begins with a series of clues that add up to reveal life isn't working out the way they'd imagined or hoped, just like it did in my own life. What they notice is a strangely counterproductive repeating pattern that stands in the way of their highest potential and ultimate sense of meaning and fulfillment. In most cases, the life built on an unexamined script ends up in a cycle of these patterns, which produce a self-fulfilling prophecy. This means that what is feared most eventually manifests. Over and over and over again.

When this happens, it's as if they have reached a plateau and their psyche just won't let them stretch enough to be the courageous person they might be if they had a bit more inner strength and confidence. Something always stops them just short of greatness. They would have everything they wanted if only this or that were possible. They begin to wonder, "Why do I keep doing what I do? Why am I so resistant to changing what I know I should? Why can't life be different?"

REFLECTION:

Take a few moments and reflect on your life thus far. How much of your life is about what someone else or society thinks you should be doing? Does this feel aligned with your deepest values? Do you have clarity about why you are here? What must you do before you leave this earth?

My Notes

Rigid vs. Agile Mindset

How do you know what to do when you realize you are living the same self-fulfilling prophecy again and again? You've realized that you are following unhealthy, repetitive life patterns. Sometimes they seem to be working, but more often they lead you to the same dead end. Maybe you've even begun to realize you have been following an unexamined life script from childhood, what I would call a FOO, or family-of-origin, story. Some people take the time to reflect and figure out where the change is needed and how to do it. And some don't. The latter strive for the next pleasure and avoid the next pain. In character science we call this the rigid or fixed mindset personality. The "I am who I am, and I don't plan to change" proclamation. "Everyone around me just needs to adjust!"

Unfortunately, it's always a cycle. It's easy to predict this mindset will create the same set of circumstances again and again. When following the unexamined script of life, people believe they are right because they have not yet learned the most important lesson in life, one they should have learned in childhood: For every action there is a consequence, and if you want a different outcome, you have to examine your actions to alter your course and get a better result. If you want to change your circumstances, chances are, what you really need to change is your perspective first, then your choices.

Indeed, there's another way to live. It requires learning to pause, be still, listen, and be open to learning. To reflect on cause and effect. We must figure out specifically what led to our outcomes and write new ones, then work backward to choose a better life. In character science we call this a growth or agile mindset.

At Tilt, we believe some traits will endure (nature traits) and others are more malleable (nurture traits) through character strength development. The ability to pause between stimulus and response is one of the most important signs of maturity and enlightened creativity. It means we continuously work to be alert to our impulses and pause to consider our intentions mindfully. We take into account our impact on others and consider our ultimate purpose. This mindset is what separates us from our reptilian nature. Reptilian impulses are an instinctive reaction to fear that ensure survival, and they become part of our automatic personality patterns. In contrast, conscious action is our response to stimulus and gives our moral character time to choose a more mindful action.

Wherever you go, your habitual patterns follow you. When life gets uncomfortable, we have an inner urge to change something, but if we don't stop to examine what caused it in the first place, the patterns that caused it will follow us into the next situation too. Our unconscious patterns shape the destiny of our life, unless we stop to examine the underlying motives of our patterns and change specific habits, one at a time.

REFLECTION:

Ask yourself why you do the things you do, even when you profess to do otherwise. Are you able to detach from your instinctual desires and impulses to examine the underlying motives and choose more intentionally? Can you delay seeking pleasure right now for something better long term? The world is full of possibilities. Why not choose the best outcome you can imagine?

My Notes

It is in our darkest moments that we must face who we are and who we want to be next.

Fight, Flee, Freeze or deFlect

Let's consider for a moment what it means to live from our most primal survival instincts, versus living by our more advanced mammalian brain.

In attempting to explain the relative contribution of nature (inherited DNA) and nurture (learned behaviors), we believe that certain traits are strongly imprinted in our DNA pattern and predispose us to certain personality tendencies and patterns that are more akin to an ability—or what some may call an innate trait or strength—and will not likely change very much over time. We agree that inborn qualities that are unique to you alone will inevitably last a lifetime and make you who you are. We call this your True Tilt Profile (visit tilt365.com), and we encourage you to amplify the energy you spend in this set of traits, as long as you don't unwittingly overuse them.

We also believe that a subset of personality traits are related to how we interpreted our earliest social relationships in our first family system, and that these may need development if the "nurture" part of our development could have gone better. This is the part of our personality and character that was largely modeled and taught to us by caregivers. This learned part of our personality is retained in the family-of-origin stories we made up about why things work the way they do in our first family system. What we learn is very useful in surviving that first social system. But it may not work as well when we go into the world at large, because circumstances and dynamics are often very different. These stories (family narratives) can certainly be tweaked and evolved. And they need to be examined every time we enter a new social system. The question is whether we let our cold-blooded reptilian nature (survival) be the guide, or choose our more advanced human capabilities to learn and grow along the way so we move beyond just survival to thrive.

Here's how it goes without the human capacity of reflection. Living like a lizard isn't all bad. Our only job is to live, eat, compete, reproduce, die. Our instincts are good at it, too. If another lizard attacks and our odds look good, we fight and win. If our odds look slim, we flee and wait for a better angle next time or slink away into submission to the new alpha lizard. If things get really bad and we're in danger of being eaten alive, we freeze and play dead. Who wants a dead lizard, after all? And last but not least, if we get caught unaware and something sticky lands on us, we simply deflect it onto someone or something else. Let them deal with the nasty goo. We just don't want it on ourselves. Yuck.

Not bad, the life of a lizard. Bigger alpha lizards get better at fighting. Lean, fast lizards get better at fleeing. Small, quiet lizards get better at hiding and freezing. And tricky, deceptive lizards get better at flipping and deflecting their stuff onto others. This is a brilliant design. In real danger, fear is a gift and keeps us from harm, so it shouldn't be ignored. Our instinctual (gut) fears can save us from danger in a split second, many times faster than our conscious brain can operate, so their value is immeasurable. We are designed the way we are for a good reason: to survive an often unfriendly environment. Tuning in to our fears can give us clues about whom and when to trust, and when not to. Your early brain learned what was good for you and what wasn't, and most of the time, it's right. With one exception . . .

What if we have aspirations to be more than just primal creatures trying to survive? Then we have to consider how our limbic, or emotional, system might believe our reptilian fears and escalate them even more if we don't learn how they work and how to manage them. Being conscious beings requires us to transcend emotional drama in order to save energy for our most creative work. Though emotions can be enormously informative, they can also sometimes feel muddled and confusing.

Some of the most deeply rooted, stubborn feelings are tied to old memories that happened before our more complex adult brain was developed. These oldest memories remain inextricably linked to instinctual fears that lie hidden and dormant until they are triggered. That's where they can catch us off guard and wreak havoc without our conscious permission. If we had a

DEFLECT
FREEZE
FLIGHT
FLEE

painful experience early in life, the feelings associated with them will arise whenever we have a new experience that feels similar. Part of ourselves that we didn't know lurked within can take over and surprise us. Our inherited nature is imprinted in our fearful reptilian brain, designed to help us survive. But our nurtured patterns can change, with the help of our more conscious mammalian brain, beyond surviving to thriving. The first step is to take a five-second pause before acting from fear, and choose to act from inner strength instead.

REFLECTION:

Are you best at fighting, fleeing, freezing, or deflecting? Be honest: When you're in a corner and feeling defensive, what instincts are the fastest go-to in your reptilian nature? Think of a time when you felt fearful but chose to wait and act from a more conscious part of yourself. Contrast the outcomes in both. Which ended in a better result?

Foe or FOO, Know the Difference.

But which fears are there for good reason and which ones should we question? That's the big question. And further, how can we attend to the value of our fears while not letting them escalate into unhealthy patterns or drama?

Let's make a simple distinction here and employ our emotions to interpret the signals. When a fear arises, the first thing we should do is notice it and tune in to it. Then test it against reality. Is there real danger possible? Is your gut telling you the person approaching you in the parking lot is not someone to trust? Then pay attention! Real danger could be afoot, and the person could be a predator. We don't want to override this kind of instinctual fear with another kind of fear that is more contrived. It's called ego fear. For example, if you have a FOO story that wired you up to be a people-pleaser in order to try to get love that was withheld in your family, you might be tempted to override your instinctual fear with ego fear and be nice to a complete stranger, putting yourself in real physical danger. Right there is the distinction. Learning to discern between instinctual fear (clues to survival) and ego fear (social strategy) is essential to thriving.

How do you know when your fears are really ego fears instead of instinctual fears? Both are wicked fast and cause you to act quickly. But the ego fears are identifiable as patterns that are good for you in moderation and potentially very bad for you in extremes, because they most often lead to drama and energy loss. There are four of them that you want to make sure are not over-played patterns, patterns that are really about unmet human needs and unanswered questions, and that can drive more of your behavior than you realize. The first is approval-seeking to meet the need for belonging. The second is status-seeking to meet the need for respect. The third is power-seeking to meet the need for independence. And the last is attention-seeking to meet the need to be special. All four are designed for our good in moderation and help us form a healthy ego. But if these needs weren't met when we were growing up, they can become treacherous and unconscious dictators of our behavior, wreaking havoc in our adult relationships. The trick is to become familiar with them, so we know what our hidden ego parts are really up to!

My Notes

40

Wasting precious energy on unconscious ego drama means less is left for one's purpose.

Your FOO is Your Responsibility

All conflict in social interactions, whether personal or professional, extends from unresolved identity (ego) issues that began in our earliest years of life. Those identity questions result in ego sensitivities that we carry into adult life. Those ego sensitivities stem from stories we made up as children, and as a result, they often have an immature storyline. We call these family-of-origin, or FOO, stories. These stories are always a little distorted by childlike perceptions. Let me explain how FOO stories unfold, just so you have the basics.

Growing up, we learn two main ego states that come from our parent-child relationships. As children we learn to comply for approval or rebel to differentiate ourselves, and both are necessary for our development. We experience our parents as the ones who are in control and who instruct and teach us, and these interactions create impressions that eventually become ego states that we either mimic or reject. Before long they are imprinted in our social styles and form our relationship to authority figures and the world at large. Think about playing "mommy, daddy, or teacher" as a child. These were our first experiences of authority and created a lasting impression about how we view authority figures forever. It looks like this:

The primary goal of the parent or caregiver is to help their children grow a positive sense of self—a strong internal identity—and to teach them how to one day behave as an adult and accomplish independence, achievement, social respect, and fulfillment. A big part of this development into adulthood means learning

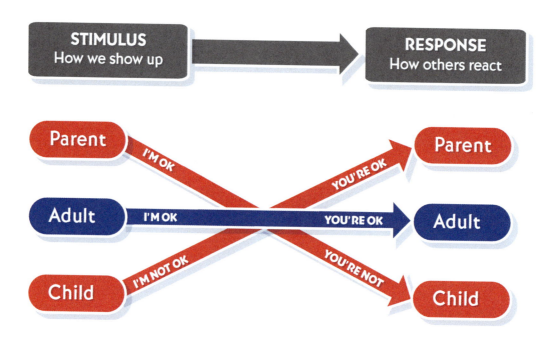

how to make connections between choices or actions and their outcomes or consequences. When early interactions lead to negative results, oftentimes those negativities are imprinted on the child. As an adult they will have to reexamine that FOO story to make it applicable to successful adulthood relationships. We are born with personalities and as we grow into adulthood, we develop character... but only if we take the time to examine our own FOO stories. Character development takes a lifetime.

We all have some level of traumatic experience as children, so most of us have our own trigger points. The solution is to learn the underlying cause—find the FOO story—rather than react with FOO stress reactions that trigger drama. That's what character is, choosing to act as a mature, professional adult in your social interactions no matter how someone else shows up.

Positive Parent = Nurturing Teacher & Champion (these feed a strong identity)
Negative Parent = Critical Parent & Controlling Parent (these discount our identity)
Positive Child = Receptive Learner & Creative Explorer (these feed our quest for growth)
Negative Child = Compliant Victim & Rebellious Escapist (these make us feel helpless)

Positive Parent Interactions call forth Good Child Reactions (and feed a strong identity).

Negative Parent Interactions call forth Negative Child Reactions (and feed low self-esteem).

Adult Identity = A positive relationship with self and others that extends from high self-esteem (identity) and character (choosing responsibility).

REFLECTION:

Have you ever been set off by someone else's actions only to find out your coworkers, friends, and peers were unable to understand why you were so upset? Try to think back on times when similar situations occurred. How did you react? If you are finding a pattern in your actions, then you were probably playing out a FOO story of your own.

How FOO Looks on the Surface

There are a list of symptoms that can give us clues that we are in a FOO story, symptoms that indicate a challenging interaction called a double bind. These situations usually lead to trouble, because they are based on a confusing world of contradictory logic. Double-bind FOO stories happen when our families taught us mixed messages that were no-win scenarios based on distorted reasoning. For example, the parent who says "You need to make your own decisions" while doing everything for you is sending a mixed message. Or even more extreme, telling you to "get along with your siblings" when they are clearly being abusive bullies. These conflicting messages don't make sense, and yet we form illogical rules in our mind about them. And record mixed feelings at the same time. Like "When people are mean and out to harm me, I must overcome my fear and be nice to them anyway." Wrong! That's a double-bind FOO story that can wreak havoc in your life for years into adulthood. It's called a double bind because neither person in the interaction is going to win, unless they have examined their FOO stories and are aware of the distorted logic they create.

What are the symptoms of a double bind? These interactions feel strangely and intensely emotional. They feel confusing and irrational. They feel more extreme than reality calls for. They feel unreasonably dangerous, but you can't put your finger on it, so they don't make sense. They feel uncomfortable. You want to fix them as soon as possible to make the feelings go away. And all the while, others around you don't understand why it's so important, and they can see reality much more clearly than you. They are not caught up in it, and think you are going a little overboard. Inside you feel a sense of urgency to do something. Now. And you can't seem to stop yourself. Yep, that's not going to end well. And somewhere deep inside, you know it.

Let's think through a real-world work example to illustrate why it's important to identify the potential for these unproductive interactions. An employee submits an important presentation to his supervisor. What the employee doesn't realize is that poor grammar or errors in work trigger a stressful reaction in his supervisor because of the supervisor's FOO story. When the supervisor was a child, her parent constantly corrected her every imperfection, and as a result the supervisor has always been hyperaware of errors. The supervisor is frustrated upon receiving what she perceives to be poorly executed work. Time is short and the work needs to be submitted soon. She feels irritation rising and wonders why a highly paid executive would submit unpolished, unfinished work to her.

However, the supervisor has examined her life script and instead of letting her FOO story take control, she takes the lead. She makes a note of the action for future reference but chooses not to get too concerned at this point. She dashes off an email. The employee gets the email, which reads, "It looks to me like you still have some work to do before this will be ready for final submission. The content here is excellent, but the polish is not there, so it appears to still be in a draft stage. Please use spell-check and grammar-correcting software before you send work along to me on future assignments, and it will shorten the back-and-forth time." The employee is devastated.

To some of you reading this, the email response sounds like a very reasonable factual statement and request. But the employee has his own unexamined FOO story. He grew up with a very critical parent who constantly discounted his worth, and the email is a major trigger point—especially considering the employee is living an unexamined life script and has never considered how this childhood experience may be influencing his adult decisions. The employee's feelings are hurt, and he goes on to call the supervisor a critical ogre behind her back. He complains to his peers about what a mean boss he has. But worst of all, the employee feels as he did when he was a child, subjected to well-intentioned but imperfect parenting. Now to make matters worse, he feels guilty and fearful about gossiping.

In a situation like this, the supervisor needs to know how to respond so that the situation doesn't escalate. Both the supervisor and employee had FOO stories. The difference is that the supervisor had taken time to examine her FOO story and knew how to make adult choices and be present with the current reality instead of getting caught up in fears about the past or future. The employee, on the other hand, had not yet examined his FOO story, and immediately began to deflect blame onto anyone but himself, because it was too uncomfortable to bear responsibility alone. Approval from his supervisor is too important to his sense of self-worth. Were he willing to consider the driving force behind his reactions, he might examine his FOO story and change from a defensive mindset to an agile mindset. Instead of feeling devastated, he could take it as a moment to learn how to do better next time. In this way, he would allow a portion of his personality to evolve through a commitment to character growth, and would choose better responses. And ultimately, better relationships too.

REFLECTION:

Think back to the reflection from the last section. Think of those instances when your reaction played off one of your own FOO stories, resulting in a negative outcome. Now try to think of something you could have done differently. Play out the scenario a couple of different ways and see if you can come up with a more positive outcome.

50

Fears you hide from yourself will show up in everything about you, and the world will believe you.

Can People Really Change?

Yes. And no. It depends on how proactive they are about self-reflection and self-regulation, which takes courage and practice. Let me break it down for you: There's a section in the prefrontal cortex of the brain that is physically larger in people who practice self-regulation versus those who simply react to whatever shows up, without pausing to reflect. This brain function has to be exercised regularly, and it's what mature adults do before they take action. They consider, they listen, they notice, they reflect, and then they respond. They can do this because they have strong self-regard and don't immediately feel defensive or offensive. I call this the five-second pause for reflection. My experience is that proactive people have an amazing capacity to create positive influence when they are more reflective and mindful of their impact.

Do you remember when I said the catalyst for avoiding the unexamined life begins with questions? Existential questions? Through my research, and my own life experiences, I've found that if an individual can answer affirmatively to eight essential questions of a healthy identity, they are more than likely able to self-regulate with ease. This is because they are not trying to get their ego needs met externally, from others, but are mindful and respect themselves on the inside. People like this are easy to be around, and we let them in to influence us because of the ease and calm we sense in them. Quite simply, they are safe to be around because they are not manipulating us with their agenda to resolve unconscious ego fears, and we can sense it.

However, some of us simply react to situations by following patterns from two versions of old, unexamined stories. The first is from an unresolved child ego state, which reacts defensively. The second is from an unresolved, over-pronounced parent superego state, which reacts offensively. This sometimes happens in children who had to grow up too fast, taking charge too early in life because of family circumstances. Both these ego states can become over-pronounced and create lots of drama in relationships, professionally and personally. Adults who operate from a child ego state are often taking less than 100% responsibility for their lives. Their mode of interaction implies "I'm not okay," so they unwittingly invite others to take charge. Adults who operate from a parent ego state are often taking more than 100% of their responsibility—taking on things that should be someone else's responsibility. The implied message is "I'm okay, you're not," so they cross boundaries trying to take charge of other adults when that is not their place.

Either of these two ego states comes from a FOO story that may have worked in our family but is often unwelcome in other adult systems we encounter later. Other adults want to be treated as equals; they want both parties to take 100% responsibility of their own part, but mind their own business about others. This confers a message of "I'm okay and you're okay, and we are both here as adults with choices at our disposal." Staying in overused child or parent ego states in adult interactions creates unbalanced adult relationships and, eventually, frustration and conflict when one or the other tires of the arrangement. Those who keep interacting from overused child states wonder why life has given them such inferior circumstances and those who operate from overused parent states think they alone are right and can save the day. Both continue to have issues in the workplace or in their personal lives, where they often feel left out, unappreciated, misunderstood, and even isolated, because their mode of interaction often creates dissonance with other healthy adults.

In these cases, the issues are a direct result of an unexamined life script that has manifested itself so greatly inside, it now manifests outside as well. When you seek to fill a hole inside by getting something from others, they feel turned off by your lack of good boundaries. Indeed, when these unexamined scripts take over, people go through life unaware of how their life script is directing their agendas—directing their lives down paths that lead away from their full creative output. What do I mean by that? The full creative output is the Providence, the goal, the destiny, the meant-to-be . . . the biggest dreams of all. But if you are too busy trying to fill an insatiable hole inside your identity, you will never have the energy or time to devote to your purpose.

But the good news is, if you are reading this book, then you are probably looking for a change. And here is the secret: The catalyst for the change needed to find and follow your own life script, to reach your full creative output, is presence. Now, let me show you how it's done.

REFLECTION:

In what ways do you show up like a compliant, resentful, or rebellious child? Are you taking less than 100% responsibility for your outcomes and giving away your power? In what ways do you show up like the controlling or critical parent? Are you taking more than 100% responsibility—responsibility for what is someone else's business—and therefore assuming more power than is yours? How might this rob others of learning to take responsibility themselves?

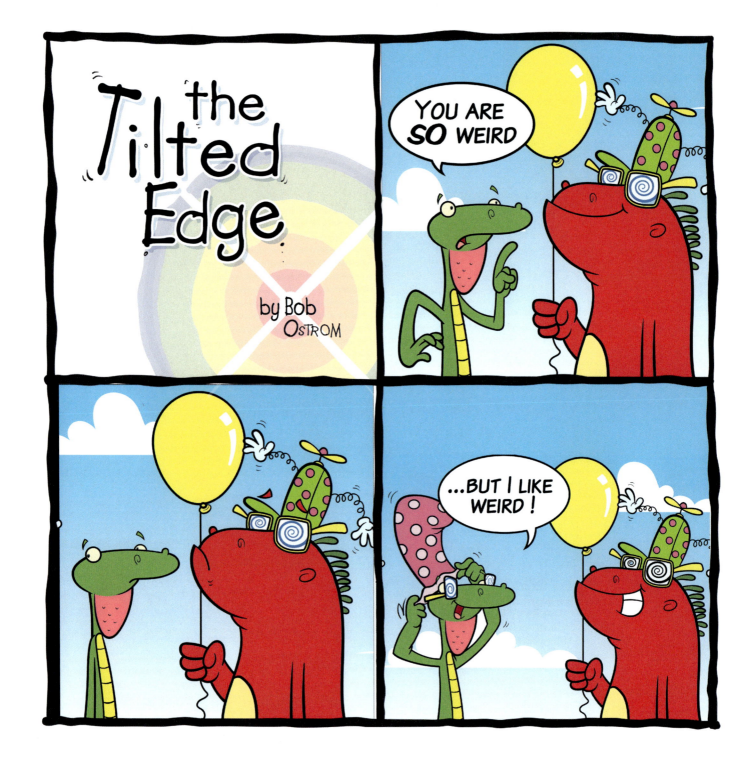

Your Inner Circle

Before we move on to discuss the path to powerful inner presence, I want to provide one caveat to successful adult interaction. There will be times when relationships need to change because they are no longer a good fit. When what one person wants from a relationship no longer works for the other, the fit has become the problem. Where we are tempted to go is to blame the other person for the problem, when actually it's the relationship between you that may have changed for one or both parties.

Life and time change us. People evolve and grow, so their wants and needs may change. The best way to handle this is to acknowledge that life is short and living in compromised relationships that only serve one of the parties will not make for happy lives. Good relations require both parties get important basic needs and wants met in the agreed partnership, whatever it is. The premise that helps us move forward when this happens is to acknowledge that neither party is to blame; both are okay in their natural right to want happiness by their own definition. What has changed is the fit of the agreement between them. If we are able to maintain this respectful mindset toward one another and process the loss responsibly on both sides, then the relationship can change or end fairly smoothly.

Yet there will also be times when you encounter someone who does not have the self-awareness to maintain adult interactions with you, even after many attempts on your part inviting them to interact in that way. This usually happens when you are a perfect match for each other's FOO stories. They trigger the one thing that annoys you most, and you trigger the one thing that annoys them most. While there is rich material here for your growing self-awareness, it doesn't mean you should choose to continue living with stressful relationships in order to do your own work. It's better that you take that personal work to a professional and get expert help.

Staying in situations that generate chronic stress is not the way to go for anyone involved. Eventually, this can be exhausting and begin to cause you too much pain and wasted energy that will take you away from your most important work and can even cause emotional and physical repercussions if you continue to stay engaged. Someone has to be the one to stop the madness, and it is wise if that someone is you. At times you may think you have no choice, as it may be your supervisor, a colleague, or perhaps a family member who will always be in your life. What is important to remember is that you have choices, some more ideal than others. It is helpful to try some experiments and see if any of them work, but definitely proceed swiftly so you don't end up with health problems from chronic stress.

The most important thing to remember is that you are the author of your own life and you are free to choose relationships that feed your soul. Your inner circle of family and friends is sacred ground, and you must choose wisely if you are to have the chance to actualize your full potential.

Option 1: Fix the fit

The optimal option is when both parties can take a break and let the fears and emotions settle down with some space and passed time. Once the fears recede, rational thinking inevitably returns, and both parties can discuss the fear-triggering situation with an adult perspective and take 100% responsibility for their own part in the interaction while letting the other party do the same. The key is to manage what you have control over—yourself. And stay out of the other person's business as much as possible. Communicate how it felt to you without making them responsible for your reactions and feelings. Tell them the story you are making up about it in your mind, so they can attempt to understand how it might have felt to you, but don't ask them to take full responsibility for any choices that belong to you. You can make a request that they do the same, but don't expect it. Think of the interaction as between two adults, both volunteers and each having the option to make different choices at any point in the future. The fit between you may have changed, but don't try to make it anyone's fault. Honestly address whether it still works and is important enough to prioritize over being right.

Option 2: Cheerful child

If the first option isn't possible because of important variables, and you choose to continue having them in your life for important reasons, it's a little more challenging. Examples would be if they were your family, your spouse or partner's family, your children's family, or work colleagues. In this case, you value the connected relationship enough to tolerate the relationships that come along with it. Perhaps you value your job enough to tolerate a difficult dynamic in someone there. The hardest one is if this person is your supervisor, because by your own choice to stay, you are giving them power over many aspects of your professional life for a time. This is why companies must ensure they do not put people in leadership roles who do not operate mostly in a healthy, adult-to-adult mode.

In any case, if you choose to stay for the other benefits involved, there are two ways to address keeping boundaries intact. The first is a "cheerful child" mindset, where you play dumb to the invitations to drama from the other person. You keep interactions to a minimum, show up to honor the other more valued relationship (perhaps going to a holiday event to support your spouse), and put on a happy, cheerful persona, doing your part to be cordial and keeping time to a minimum. This works best in short interactions and allows you to focus on what you do value more. You're tolerating some inconvenience to have something bigger. The key is to avoid taking the bait and doing the drama dance with them yet again. What works better is to keep interactions superficial and polite. Keep in mind that they are not your inner circle, but they are to some other important person or entity to which you are committed.

Option 3: Closed parent

The other option you have when previous attempts don't work is to move to a "closed parent" mode and assert your boundaries—clearly, succinctly, and most importantly, through your actions. When others won't listen and keep trying to pull you into unconscious FOO patterns that are stressful for you, it may be time to say no by stopping the interaction entirely. Why? Because the dynamic is highly likely to continue in the same vein it has proven to in the past. And that is not good for anyone. The best predictor of future behavior is past behavior, for the most part. In this case, you must exercise some parent ego state in yourself and find the courage to say no to relationships that don't feed your best self at this time. If you can live without the relationship, just exercise your power, step into parent mode, and make it clear that you do not want to continue the relationship because it isn't good for you right now. In this case the best choice is to simply remove yourself. Do nothing. Don't interact. Force an end to the madness. Then take your inner work to an expert who can help you sort it out. Wish the other person well and be open to crossing paths later when things have changed.

Now that we have clarity about what can drain your energy, let's look at what can power it up. Sometimes saying no is more important than saying yes. Every ounce of your energy will be required to finish your creative work in the world, so it is up to you to evaluate your inner circle and make conscious choices about what you choose. The key is to remember you are the one who is free to choose your inner circle.

REFLECTION:

Do an inventory of your inner circle at work and in your personal life. Who supports and feeds your best self? Who doesn't? Are there any relationships you need to address with some of the options posed in this chapter? Are you in a position to funnel the majority of your energy into your creative work and unique purpose in the world?

My Notes

Pruning the weak limbs of our old patterns, though painful, becomes worth it as we grow stronger and bear more fruit.

8 Questions
check list

1: ☐ YES ☐ NO: **Am I safe?** (Security vs. Mistrust)

2: ☐ YES ☐ NO: **Am I capable?** (Power vs. Self-Doubt)

3: ☐ YES ☐ NO: **Am I good?** (Approval vs. Rejection)

4: ☐ YES ☐ NO: **Am I special?** (Attention vs. Guilt/Shame)

5: ☐ YES ☐ NO: **Am I important?** (Status vs. Insignificance)

6: ☐ YES ☐ NO: **Am I productive?** (Autonomy vs. Dependence)

7: ☐ YES ☐ NO: **Am I valued?** (Acceptance vs. Isolation)

8: ☐ YES ☐ NO: **Am I worthy?** (Recognition vs. Despair)

The Eight Essential Questions

One of the key domains in developmental psychology is the formation of an identity that creates presence. When a person is truly present, they tend to exude presence. They possess the internal agility to contextualize swiftly and pause to consider the moral implications of their actions. I have found that by choosing behavior that is in alignment with the timeless principles of good moral character, people tend to increase their own experiences of happiness and fulfillment. I've listened to hundreds of life stories and collected research on thousands of adults who report higher levels of life and work satisfaction, engagement, and creativity when they can give affirmative answers to eight existential questions.

Building on research conducted by Erik Erikson, Eric Berne, Carl Jung, Carol Pearson, Ken Wilbur, and other great thinkers in the domain of human development, I posit that the eight questions in this book can increase our grasp of reality as we grow over time. During our journey, we may pass some questions over in favor of others, only to come back to those we missed when the time is right. From years of qualitative research, I've noticed that we often circle back to unresolved questions of identity and polish them off when the opportunity or motivation naturally arises, creating another level of self-growth. Our psyche also appears to create conflicts and dilemmas that invite us to resolve them even when we are not aware of it consciously.

I've also conducted quantitative research on accelerating this growth of awareness, supported by practices we have adopted in executive coaching, using assessments and exercises that educate executives about the eight questions that must be answered affirmatively for strong influential presence. My experience is that if a client is successful in doing the personal work to generate positive answers (building evidence to validate maturation through experiences), the growing body of evidence can become the engine that drives healthy, adult ego and creates a solid internal compass by which to steer. This enables them to move beyond unconscious, biased personality preferences and acting out on fearful impulses, to non-dualistic agility and resourceful creativity that extends from inner character strength. In these times of flow, clients also tend to be more socially generative than those who spin around in distortions of reality and waste precious energy in service of unresolved ego strivings and FOO fantasies.

REFLECTION:

Do you sometimes notice people pushing you away or avoiding you? When this happens, make notes about what transpired just before this happened. Were you trying to get something from them? Push an agenda, get them to take care of a need you have? Force, persuade, or manipulate them into your way of thinking? Insist that you are right? Seduce them with your charm to pull them back? Notice that while you may have short-term success, you ultimately lose them in the long run. How can you show up calmer and more at ease with their freedom of choice, presenting the facts and letting them choose for themselves?

My Notes

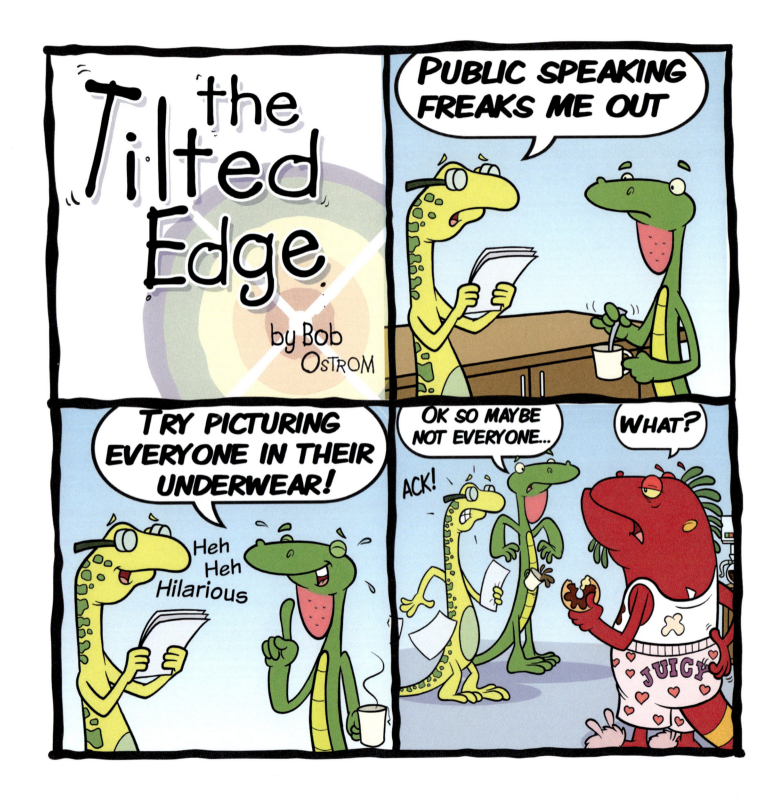

The Path to Rock Solid Presence

So, how does it work? You have the basic ideas, now on to the questions you must answer to have rock-solid internal self-regard and external presence (even in a stress-filled world full of noise).

In the first twenty or so years of life we must resolve the first four questions to become independent adults. Two are easy for us, because of predisposed personality patterns handed down through DNA, and two are sometimes more challenging, because they are less natural for our tendencies. But here's the good news: The two questions that are yours to solve are not necessarily the same for others. That's what makes it all doubly confusing and frustrating in a complex social world, but also allows us to complement one another. Others seem to do what we cannot, and they do it with ease. That's also why we are attracted to them. Our two questions are the ones that are more difficult for them, which is where the trouble can begin if we don't understand and appreciate each other. So it carries on throughout life if we don't know what drives our behavior and keep repeating our unresolved identity fears. We keep attracting the same people, to get into the same conflicts, rather than resolving the dilemma once and for all so our relationships are more mutually fulfilling.

These eight questions will show you how to become a self-aware, enlightened version of yourself. It will make what you need to resolve absolutely clear. If your answer to any of them is a resounding no, then hiring a professional to help you is the way to go. In some cases this can involve therapy, but I have found that most business executives are intelligent and resourceful about growth. If you engage a Master Tilt Coach, they can help you use character strengths and your true self to understand the less-developed, fear-based parts inside you. Doing the work can change your patterns and relationships for life, enabling you to transcend your unconscious fears (yes, you have them) and choose courage.

The first four questions are meant to be resolved in the first two decades of life, in the first round of development. Then you circle back to expand on them, over and over in the life cycle, to further polish them in a continuous spiral of growth that becomes the trajectory of your legacy. These first four are very basic to the development of positive social interactions. If our answer to one or more of these first four questions is no, then we will have trouble in an adult world with the development task of that question and will operate from distortions (FOO stories) that are based on the interpretations of a child. You will know you are in one when the world feels a little bit like Alice in Wonderland and nothing makes sense. You know in your rational mind you shouldn't feel the way you do, but there it is!

FOO stories were made up in a child's mind, so they are not based on facts and adult reasoning. When one of them is left unresolved, we will look everywhere in the world to resolve it. For example, if we have been told that children are to be seen and not heard, we may look everywhere for places to have a voice but contradict that innate desire by being silent instead. This may have helped us cooperate with our primary caregivers, but imagine how that might not serve us very well much later in life. That's huge. And it's why we can't just let FOO stories sit unresolved. But first we need a little clarity about the first four questions and development tasks. Then I will share some of our methods for resolving them swiftly, with evidence-based development, and building rock-solid presence in your real self. Let's begin!

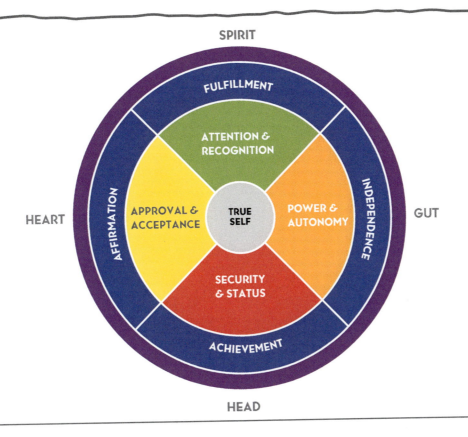

REFLECTION:

Take a first look at the Tilt Presence Wheel here. The first four questions, presented next, will help you understand the first four tasks of whole-person identity. If these four tasks are developed well in your early years of life, you will enter the world of adults from a strong sense of self. If you encountered less than optimal experiences from well-intended caregivers in your first social system, these will help you operate from presence and interact positively with others most of the time. As you read the next four sections, make reflection notes for yourself about each of the four core parts of mature adult identity.

Do your fears have you, or do you have them? Knowing who you are means the rudder of your life is in good, strong hands.

Question #1
☐ Am I safe?
(Security vs. Mistrust)

The underlying need is to experience a reasonable sense of safety in our first relationships. "Can I trust that my caregivers will appropriately prioritize my needs to help me survive?" This requires self-sacrifice on the caregivers' part.

Development age: 0–18 months

Significant relationship: Mother, father, caregivers

Developmental task: Security with authority figures

Unconscious fear: I am inferior to others who are in control

Dilemma: Security vs. mistrust

Four Outcomes

Emotional: Secure attachment—"I feel emotionally safe"

Intellectual: Communication established—"I feel understood"

Physical: Protection is noticed—"I feel protected physically"

Spiritual: Hope is established—"My free spirit is appreciated"

One of the first four developmental tasks of our instinctual nature is to seek safety, security, and comfort. Our learning objective is to assess whether the world is a safe place or a frustrating, unpredictable, or even dangerous place. If our basic needs are satisfied by our primary caregivers after reasonable effort on our part, we decide that others are trustworthy and we form a healthy attachment and connection. If our caregivers are anxious, we might believe there's a good reason to be anxious, just because they are, and have trouble trusting the idea that we are going to be okay. If they neglect us, then we may surmise that it's difficult to get the attention needed to survive and may adapt by trying different methods to get what we need. A child may mal-adapt by resisting their need of the caregiver and form an avoidant attachment. Or they may mal-adapt by being fearfully demanding and form an insecure attachment. In the worst case, they may form a disorganized attachment and later have trouble trusting others entirely.

If caregivers are unpredictable, we can become extremely stressed as infants. And if neglected or abused to the extreme, we may even shut off our limbic brain (emotional center) entirely and a pattern of instinctual manipulation will set in for life, causing pathology and robbing us of our higher-order human capacities, possibly forever. This is perhaps the most important time in our developmental lives. We must learn to balance healthy mistrust with healthy trust. And the only way it will happen is if we have reasonably healthy parents who are not using their children to meet their own unsatisfied ego needs and who are wise enough to set aside some of their own ambitions on our behalf while we figure things out and mature over time.

How does all this affect us later in life? I've had clients who trust others too much and clients who don't trust others much at all. These two reactions are extremes on a continuum that caused them relationship problems all their lives. All of us shut down certain emotions at times when they are too hard to bear, but as we grow stronger, our hearts melt and come back to us through life experiences.

One executive I worked with was obsessive to the extreme. He had to control everything and everyone he encountered because of a deep-seated belief that people cannot be trusted. His insistence on perfecting every detail made everyone around him feel micromanaged, not even trusted with minor tasks. I didn't need to hear the story of his life to know what had caused this mindset. He had experienced either unpredictable or neglectful parenting early in life and circumstances had made him feel fundamentally unsafe in the world. When faced with this first dilemma, his answer was "No, people cannot be trusted and the world is unsafe." It's no wonder he elected to be a litigation attorney for a major financial corporation. His unanswered question was the underlying driver for his entire career.

His belief? "The world is bad. I must also be bad, because no one wanted to take care of me." And so everywhere he looked, he saw what was bad, wrong, neglectful, or imperfect and sought to control it to allay his own unconscious fear that he must single-handedly change those circumstances. But of course this created a self-fulfilling prophecy. The less he trusted others, the more it affected his mindset and how he interacted with others. His worst fears were doomed to repeat over and over, as his own approach caused others to believe he was the one who was not to be trusted. After all, if you can't do something for yourself, you certainly can't do it for others. They believed what he conveyed through his unspoken beliefs, that people are not to be trusted and obsessive control is the only way to prevent disaster.

Fortunately, he was enormously intelligent, and while I was working with him, the light came on. He understood how this early life experience kept him in his most primal, stress-induced state, and he no longer wanted to live in a chronic state of obsession about control. I worked with him to build evidence that some people could be trusted sometimes, and some people could not be trusted sometimes, but the ultimate question had to be resolved inside himself, not externally. Did he trust himself to be the judge in each context? When he could honestly answer in the affirmative reality of his accumulated wisdom, he had to let go of his reptilian need to control. The answers he had to the other six questions were more positive, albeit somewhat hindered by the crippling effect of his obsession on the two questions most foundational to social success. He decided to be less black and white; he embraced that each situation should be judged by its own merits and facts. And over time he began to trust his inner wisdom to discern situations one by one, along the way.

Once he got it, he began to soar socially and professionally. He just needed to have empathy for his own early experience and trust more in his hard-earned adult wisdom. He went back to his parents to ask about the family lore from this time in his life. It was no surprise to me to learn his mother had been extremely depressed after losing her own mother a month before he was born. Despite her best efforts, she was not emotionally available to him and could barely get out of bed herself. His father traveled all the time, so most of his foundational experience in the first few years of life was determined by a rather strict and unbending nanny who showed very little love or nurturing.

And so it began. His perception was formed during a time when he was in his reptilian mode. His first instincts were determined early. He shut down his own emotions and demanded others meet his needs, using aggressive and persistent means. And good thing he did, or he might not have lived to the next stage of life. That's the beauty of the amazing design of our psyche—it gives us what we need to survive specific situations. But those situations can change. My client's mom slowly improved and was able to heal, taking over from the nanny and being there for him, so the later periods of his life made up for the early ones. This is probably why he was so successful in his career. Work is the safest place to be if you want to avoid emotions. But that limitation wasn't enough for his greater aspirations later.

Ideal balance

You are generally trustworthy and trust others for the most part too, unless you have evidence that someone should not be trusted, and then you respond with appropriate discernment and accountability in your actions with other adults.

Practice

If you answered no to this question, here's a practice that can shift how you show up and open the way for better social connection. Imagine a bubble around you that is a safe haven. For a week, imagine that anytime anyone else comes into that bubble with you, it is your job to help them feel safe. Watch what happens and keep records of what you notice. This method can work rapidly to establish new ways of interacting that come from your real self instead of the reptilian and limbic reaction of obsession about control.

REFLECTION:

What is your answer to this question? Is the world safe? Are others safe? Are they trustworthy? Do they respond appropriately to your reasonable requests? If not, do you demand too much from them, striving to answer this question inside yourself? Are you trustworthy? Are you safe for them, or do you unwittingly harm them with your extreme demands?

My Notes

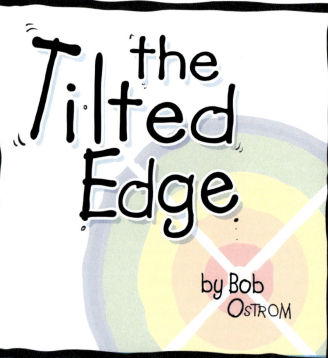

Question #2
☐ Am I Capable?
(Power vs. Self-Doubt)

The underlying need is to experience a reasonable sense of power in our first relationships. Do my caregivers let me experience an appropriate level of control over myself? This requires encouragement of graduated levels of independence on the caregivers' part.

Development age: 2-4 years

Significant relationship: Father, mother, caregivers

Developmental goal: Take initiative

Fear: I am vulnerable to others who are more powerful

Dilemma: Initiative or self-doubt

Four Outcomes

Emotional: My emotions are respected when I take action

Intellectual: My will feels respected when I take action

Physical: My boundaries feel respected when I take action

Spiritual: My freedom feels respected when I take action

The second of the four developmental tasks in strong internal ego identity is to seek power and autonomy through exploration of the world. If our parents were supportive of our explorations and let us learn how to interact with the world in a reasonable manner, then we gained a sense of agency over ourselves. This begins to form an early belief that physical interaction with things and people is something we are capable of doing. Within this identity task lies the first inklings that we are separate from our caregivers. And that we can act on our own free will.

One of the most important tasks in this development period is to make a connection between action and consequence. If our caregivers are overly controlling about our safety, then they may try to control too much of our experience and may impede our learning. For example, if a caregiver never lets you touch anything hot, you might never learn the painful consequence of that interaction. If this happens too often, the caregiver is actually teaching the child that they will not be okay without help and can't initiate action to learn for themselves, which ultimately impedes a sense of independence and competence.

The way this can play out later in life is through a deep sense of inadequacy in terms of one's capacity to interact without help. This can cause a number of distorted behaviors to appear in adult life. Some will decide to remain dependent forever and always find others who are stronger than they are to take care of them. In a way, they never grow up and remain in a compliant, resentful child ego state for life. Some people will go along with it, and take care of them. As long as that agreement stays intact, both will cooperate and be codependent. All too often, one of the parties in the relationship gets fed up with being the "parent" or the "child" and friction will arise. As one or the other grows healthier, the deal they struck may not work anymore. This usually results in constant conflict or the demise of the relationship.

The reaction to overly controlling caregivers can also have a reverse effect, as in the example of a client of mine. She was the workaholic executive who is in the office all the time, never taking a break or separating herself from her work life. Of course, she knew she should balance things out and spend more time with her family, and she kept saying she would. Her devices ruled her existence and she never left home without them. Then one day her husband announced he was involved with someone else. Someone who paid him more attention had "suddenly" stolen her life. When I met her, she shared custody of her kids with her ex and his new girlfriend, and she was horrified at the influence this woman had begun to have over her children without her permission. She had no time or desire to get back into the dating scene and felt deeply alone when her kids were at their dad's. "How did this happen?" she wondered. "Why didn't I notice the gravity of what I was potentially losing?" These are the questions that came up in her coaching sessions with me.

This is the reverse reaction to overly controlling parenting. I could guess that my client had overly cautious parents who were afraid for her to be independent and who unwittingly had a negative impact on her sense of autonomy. My client's reaction to this overly controlling behavior was to exert even more autonomy and power over her life to compensate for the fears planted in her early psyche. Thus she adapted by striving even more for the power and autonomy she needed to be an adult. Her fearful child ego state somehow believed her caregivers' message—that she wasn't capable. So, she spent all of her waking hours trying to prove them wrong, when actually it was her own beliefs about herself that needed to be edited and evolved now that she'd grown.

When I listened to her life story, sure enough, she had a worried mother who controlled her by sharing her own fears about not measuring up. Her mom had been a stay-at-home mom who didn't believe in herself and therefore could not fathom life being any different for her daughter. Fortunately, as I began to work with my client on building a case of evidence for her amazing capabilities, the falsehood of the early belief about herself began to fade. In its place she was able to see the inventory of power and autonomy she had exerted in her life and was able to shift her belief in herself on this question.

Ideal Balance:

You are generally independent and can take care of yourself, but you also recognize that interdependence is even better. You operate on the assumption that others in your life should be able to take care of themselves, too, unless they are children or otherwise physically or mentally unable to do so. Your interaction with others is healthy and balanced, in that you and others contribute by acting in service of yourself, them, and the relationship.

Practice:

If you answered no to this question, here's a practice that can shift how you show up and open the way for balanced interdependence. Follow the general rule of thumb that you shouldn't do for others what is actually their responsibility, unless you are doing so as a gift and are explicit about that. Notice if you feel an egalitarian flow in the give-and-take of the relationship, or does it feel out of balance? Don't keep score, just generally notice the mutuality of the interchange. Does it feel just right for both sides?

REFLECTION:

What is your answer to this question? Are you capable? Able to be independent? Are you overly independent? Do others give you the freedom to act on your own behalf? Do they support you when you truly need support? If not, do you demand too much from them, striving to answer this question inside yourself? Do you do more for others than you should?

My Notes

Comparison of self to others is only wise when it inspires us to imagine a better future self.

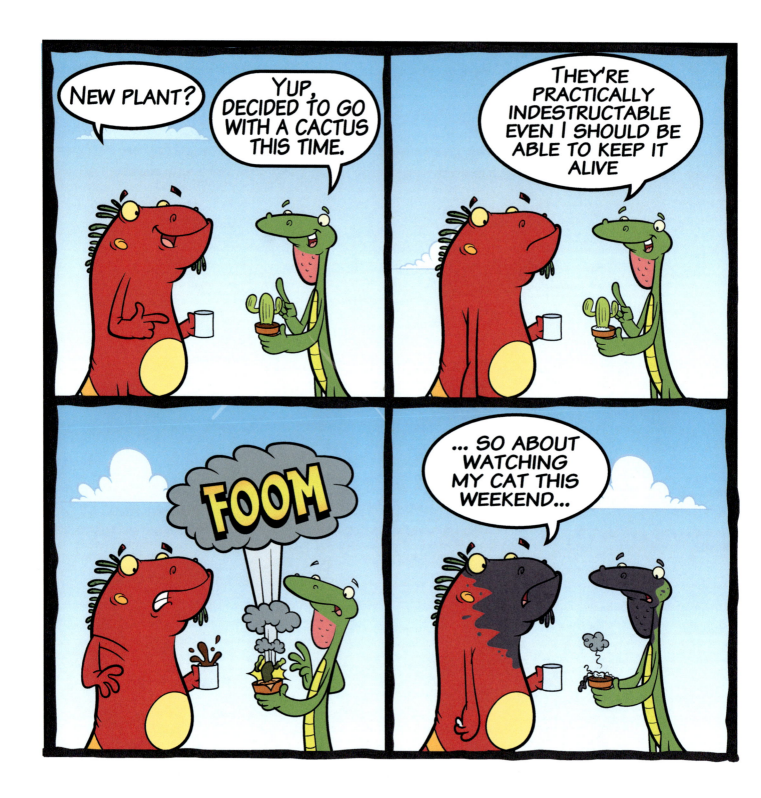

Question #3
☐ Am I good?
(Approval vs. Rejection)

The underlying need is to experience a reasonable sense of Approval in our first relationships. Do my caregivers reflect that they believe I am a good person/child despite my sometimes challenging aspects? This requires a comfortable demeanor and positive mirroring on the caregivers part for all of our emotions, not just the positive ones. For example, if the caregiver feels that being angry is "bad" and judges an infant or child for having these emotions, they are essentially rejecting an aspect of humanness in the child.

Developmental Age 4-5 years

Significant Relationship: Parents, Friends, Caregivers

Goal: Self-esteem about being lovable

Fear: Abandonment by others

Dilemma: Acceptance or rejection

Four Outcomes:

Emotional: My emotions feel mostly accepted by others.

Intellectual: My communications feel mostly accepted by others.

Physical: My physical actions feel mostly accepted by others.

Spiritual: My free spirit feels mostly accepted by others.

The third of the four initial tasks of identity in our childhood is to accept our humanness and accept all of our human qualities, pleasant or unpleasant as they are to our caregivers. Many parents, for example, were conditioned by their own parents to believe that being good means never being sad or angry. These emotions, though human, are sometimes uncomfortable for parents to experience in their children. If caregivers react by rejecting some emotions and rewarding others, the child will begin to reject very important emotions that exist to help them. For example, the emotion of anger arises when there is a perceived injustice by someone they care about. This emotion serves them by igniting action and assertiveness required to make things right. In short, every emotion serves some important purpose in humans, and if we reject part of our humanness, we will be plagued with a view that we are somehow "bad" in our identity. In other words, we "buy" our caregivers view of us, hook, line and sinker in the early years, then pass it on to our own children later.

Consider, for example, a client I worked with who carried this burden in his identity to such an extent that he allowed himself to be taken advantage of by even those closest to him. He came to coaching about his career which had been in a plateau for several years. His complaint was a general sense of apathy and low self-confidence. When I heard his whole story, I realized that his career problems were simply another symptom of what was transpiring in his personal relationships. A kind and gentle man, he had dutifully taken care of his family for decades and he was the sole financial provider. He felt unappreciated and ignored by his wife and even more so by his son and daughter who interacted with him as if he were a bank. They were nice when they needed money and ignored him when they didn't. This behavior was probably learned by observing their mother's behavior toward him. As we worked through his sense of self and talked through the four questions, it became clear that he was struggling with the question "Am I a good person?" and was plagued by the dilemma between validation and guilt. His belief was that in order to be a good husband and dad, he was required to dutifully provide as much as they demanded, no matter how much, and with very little positive reinforcement back to him. His own family had learned to use guilt as the lever to manipulate him into giving them whatever they needed or wanted. He gladly went along for many years, as this synced up with how his parents had conducted a long and happy marriage. But what was different in this case, was an apparent unwillingness on his wife's part to truly be a partner for him in return. Instead she turned the kids against him and used his guilt to prevent him from divorcing her many years after the positive aspects of the marriage were over. It took him a while to begin to reframe his beliefs and recognize that a healthy relationship requires both parties to contribute in ways that are mutually satisfying or it becomes destructive for everyone.

  Thankfully, he slowly began to collect evidence that he was indeed a good person, even if he stopped over-providing financially for his spouse and grown children. He succeeded in getting closure, filed for divorce, agreed to a reasonable alimony payment and began to build a new life, trusting that he could eventually rebuild relationships with his children on new terms. Not long after that he was promoted into a role that played to his strengths and he began to thrive again. Claiming his courage and assertiveness enabled him to believe in his own value inside himself. Letting go of the pattern of guilt would take a long time, but by redefining what merits guilt and what does not, we collected evidence that he had nothing factual to feel guilty about. Only then did he stop over-using generosity to satisfy his need for approval beyond reason. Then he started valuing himself, giving himself that which others can never fulfill no matter how much they try. His self-respect and positive self-regard came back. His confidence came back as he owned the right to feel dissatisfied with being used by people who choose to take advantage of his positive traits. He even looked different and became the strong man he had once been by resolving the inner conflict inside him. Then shining on the outside.

Ideal Balance: We are each responsible for ourselves and can choose to contribute to the lives of others in healthy balanced ways. Both or all parties in relationships are equally responsible for contributing their part and trading skills. If we betray one another intentionally or commit crimes, then our guilt is legitimate and helps us understand that we need to fix our own behavior. However, feeling guilty for not doing what another person wants us to do for them, with no respect for our own rights in the relationship, is out of balance

Practice: Think about the purpose of guilt. Look up the definition of the word. Make a list of legitimate reasons to feel guilt. Next make a list of what makes you feel guilty. Is there anything on the list that doesn't belong there? Think back over your life to a time when you felt guilty as a child. Was the infraction really worth the feelings it called forth? Have you spent years of your life searching for reasons to feel guilty?

REFLECTION:

What is your answer to this question? Do you believe you are fundamentally a good, compassionate, empathetic person? Do you care about others and the unintended consequences of your actions that may affect them? Are you likable and generally find others likable for the most part as well?

My Notes

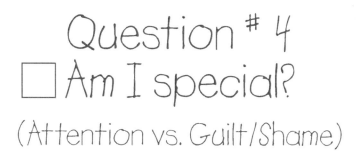
Question #4
☐ Am I special?
(Attention vs. Guilt/Shame)

The underlying need is to experience being different from our caregivers and feel that we are special to them just the way we are. Do my caregivers see me as separate from them, so that I have my own sense of uniqueness? This requires appreciation of our individual qualities, which may be different than our caregivers'.

Development age: 5–12 years
Significant relationship: Parents, teachers, friends, neighbors
Goal: Attention as a separate being that is unique
Fear: Being trapped or constrained by others

Four Outcomes
Emotional: My emotions are different and it's okay
Intellectual: My thoughts are different and it's okay
Physical: My body is different and it's okay
Spiritual: My spirit is different and it's okay

The fourth of the identity questions that enable us to get to adulthood in one piece is about claiming our individuality and uniqueness, apart from our caregivers. The human quality of novelty-seeking is the part of our identity that generates our creativity, resourcefulness, and hopeful spirit. The childlike quality of open curiosity and wonder is something that needs to be nurtured in growing children so caretakers don't unwittingly break their spirit. The quest for hope is what makes children want to learn and continue growing all their lives. This is the child who asks "Why?" about everything and endlessly seeks answers to every question that comes to mind. One can imagine that this endless learning and playing could be uncomfortable for some caregivers, who have their own lives to live, especially if they work all day. It's a balancing act for caregivers to avoid crushing their child's spirit while still managing their constant energy and enthusiasm for life. And again, like the other three identity needs, it can set up problematic behaviors if things don't go well.

Some caregivers don't give their children the freedom to become their own unique person but rather put constraints on things they don't understand or don't support. When a child shows initiative, caregivers hopefully respond with appropriate interest in order for the children to continue pursuing their own voice in the world.

Or the opposite can also occur, when parents try to live their own unmet dreams vicariously through the life of their child. If the parents were unable to express their unique skills in their own family, they may be tempted to encourage their kids to do what they did not, for example, encouraging them to play a sport or perform an art that was left unexpressed in their own life. If overdone, the parents' excessive need can feed the narcissistic aspects of the ego of the child and boost it to unrealistic levels. This serves to pump them up in a superficial way, making them believe anything is possible and overinflating the ego to feel special. If not age-appropriate, this can inflate their ego to a point of grandiosity and have a negative effect on their grounding, focus, and stability. In short, the parents can create an exaggerated sense of power and freedom that is beyond what a child should feel. This can lead them to an artificial sense of omnipotence that can lead to disappointments later in life.

Another problem often seen in parenting is the practice of complimenting a child for what they cannot control. For example, offering praise for inherited traits like good looks or for elite circumstances, which implies they are better than others. It is much better to reward the positive choices they make or accomplishments that come from hard-earned effort. In this way, parents can reinforce what builds character rather than feed the narcissistic tendencies of infancy. Children need self-focused tendencies to survive early life, but entirely selfish notions will not serve them well as they grow into adults.

An example of the dilemma of attention versus shame is illustrated by a client I coached in Silicon

Valley. A founder and optimistic visionary of a startup, this client hired me to "fix" her team, which she felt was not optimistic enough and unable to understand the sense of urgency required to pull off the expectations of the board. She was obviously quite brilliant; she'd had a great idea and managed to quickly get a first round of funding at three million dollars, and was preparing to seek a second round at ten million.

After interacting with her team, I became aware that the story of success was not matched by the facts under the surface. It seemed like my client believed her own tale and had a skill for changing the subject when someone called her on the details that didn't add up. While her enthusiastic vision had gotten them this far, problems had begun to plague the early-stage company. Turnover was high, direct reports on her leadership were divided, and the board was beginning to press in with demands to perform on tough timelines. When she approached me, she was anxious, frenetic, experiencing chronic insomnia, and had even begun to doubt the viability of the business herself. She complained about the team, wanting me to fix the naysaying and "get them on board" so they could get their next round of funding.

My sense of the situation was that the identity question "Am I special?" was at the root of this escalated dynamic, which was her desperate search to resolve the dilemma of attention versus shame. When this dilemma is left unresolved, it often plays out in a show of grandiosity, where the person seeks to be in the limelight, to be so special, they attempt to pull off the impossible—the maverick who beats the odds and does what everyone says can't be done. This is an important human quality, and sometimes by sheer enthusiasm, we do manage to accomplish unusual feats. But in this case, I feared the over-inflation of the founder's ego had made her believe she could do something that was not grounded in good research or even in the realm of reality. It seemed the vision was too unrealistic to be feasible, given the constraints and known obstacles. Half of her team had lost faith in the vision. Sensing that this might be true for her as well, I asked how certain she was that

success was imminent. Her hesitation at answering told me she was in conflict with herself. With a few more questions, I realized that she had painted herself into a corner by taking a large amount of funding from investors, and now she felt stuck and wanted out. Being a startup founder myself, I understood this dilemma well and had some experience to contribute.

The work we did together was to help her ground herself in the facts and stop exaggerating and spinning stories not based on sufficient and reasonable research. As she did her homework and dug into the details, she realized she didn't need to feel shame for not being extra special, and was able to revise the strategy and goals of the startup to pivot to a more realistic business model. She started listening to her team and answering their questions honestly, letting them help her instead of trying to persuade them with fabricated stories. Once she was more in integrity with reality and the facts, she began to have more confidence in herself and her team. They began to trust her more and began to believe in the future vision, lowering turnover and increasing real goal achievement. The result? She began to trust herself to do her homework and speak truthfully. She even called off the next round of fundraising to do more research, to ensure she could truly pull off her vision in reality.

Ideal balance
When we experience a reasonable amount of attention, we are able to find our own voice and express it in the world. If we don't get enough attention, we may find ourselves striving to get it from others but feeling there is never enough. If we get too much attention, we may feel superficial, like we are not quite ourselves, because our sense of self is puffed up beyond reason by the dreams of those we want to please.

Practice
Make a list of your dreams and lifelong goals. Are they reasonable goals given your background, resources, skills, and education? If our dreams are so big they are completely out of reach, we will inevitably grow frustrated and disillusioned. If we are sensible but push for a stretch, then we have a better chance of accomplishing our vision. Close your eyes and imagine how you will feel, look, and be when you achieve a goal. Then break it down into chunks that you can work toward one step at a time. Give yourself a timeline that is reasonable and then focus on it intently every day. Don't let yourself get caught up in voicing dreams and spinning stories that are unachievable. All this will do is make you feel like a fraud and sink your self-esteem.

REFLECTION:

Do you feel you get enough attention and recognition? Are you free to explore your own voice in the world and express it? Are your ideals overinflated, or reasonable and balanced by reality and focus? Do you notice that parts of yourself strive too much for attention and then you feel shame about needing it? Do you exaggerate stories just to make an impression, because you secretly feel you are not that special?

100

The awakening of your unique creative purpose arises only if you dive head first into the abyss of your existential angst and questions.

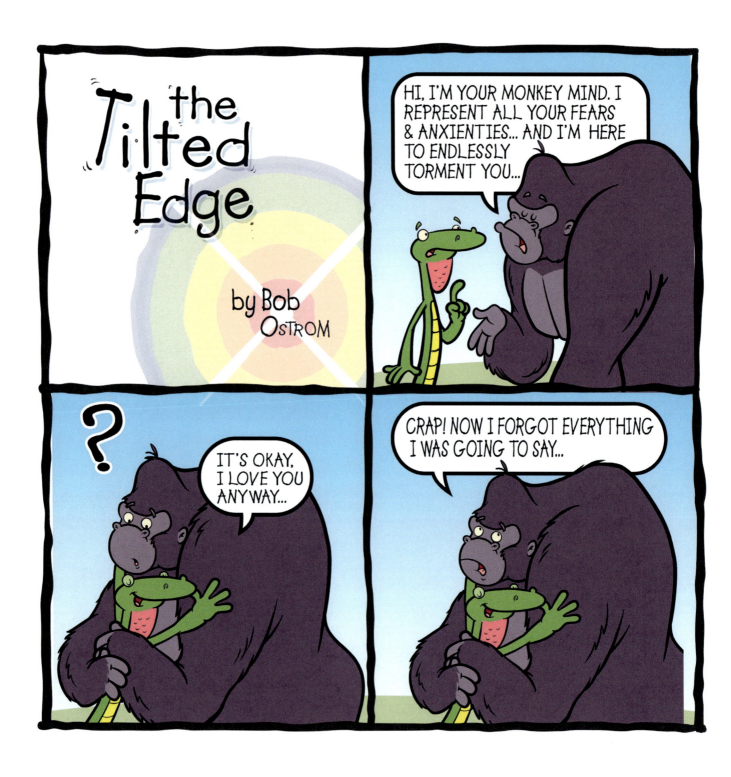

You are the final judge of you.

Once you can say yes to the four questions we've already discussed, you are able to interact with the world from a stronger internal compass based on honest self-knowledge. Until then, you will only dabble in the goals of the next four and will recreate the same dilemmas over and over until they are resolved. This is why midlife crises occur. We can only live a self-fulfilling prophecy so many times without waking up to the reality of our own making. But once we do, our life begins to show real, tangible progress for us and others in our lives.

Before we proceed with the second layer of identity tasks as we continue to grow, I want to be clear that the essential questions must be answered by you alone, inside yourself. What happens outside yourself is the external manifestation of your inner beliefs about yourself. In other words, whatever you believe about yourself will be what others believe. The most important thing to remember is that you get to decide if you are enough. No amount of praise, acknowledgment, appreciation, feedback, recognition, money, or awards can mark the check in that box for you. If you seek to have someone else or something external answer that question for you, what you will learn is that it's an insatiable hole. No amount of external recognition can measure up to your own assessment of yourself. The judgment you place on yourself may be the most important decision of your life. You know yourself more than anyone else. If your answers are not affirmative, commit to doing the work to sort them out.

When you take action to prove something to yourself, no one can take that accomplishment away from you. By taking that action, you have increased your own respect for yourself. It's kind of like the first book I wrote. I did it for me, to prove I could, and to my own level of satisfaction. If I had decided I would only give myself credit if my book was a best-seller, then the effort would have been wasted, and I would never have felt the satisfaction that comes with internal mastery. This world is full of external motivators, and that's part of the problem. In a transparent world where there is so much comparison, there will always be someone who is better. So, decide for yourself and answer your own questions inside yourself. Operate from an internal locus of control and choose what matters most to you alone.

So if you're ready, let's proceed and see where you are with the next four existential questions of identity. If you answer these affirmatively, you will join those whose lives make this world a better place.

REFLECTION:

Refer to the Tilt Presence Wheel presented on the following page. To what extent is each question resolved inside you so it doesn't feel like a need you are striving for anymore? This is your baseline for further self-exploration and provides clues to what's next in your psycho-social development.

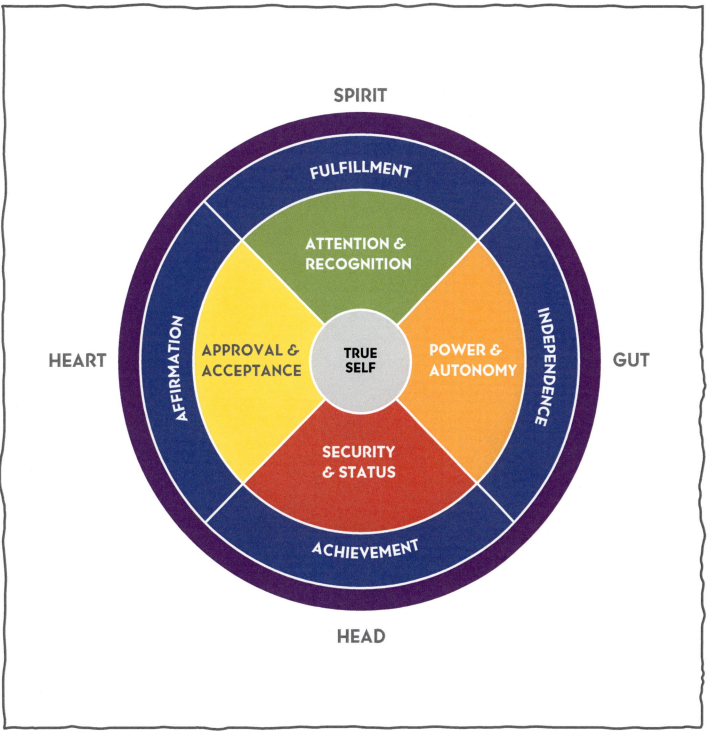

Question #5
☐ Am I important?
(Status vs. Insignificance)

The underlying need is to experience being significant and important in your domains of choice and to feel you have earned respect. This requires moving beyond feeling safe in the world, to establishing your status and achievement to your own standards.

Significant relationships: Father, teachers, peers, mentors
Goal: Status and achievement
Fear: Inferiority

Four Outcomes
Emotional: My feelings are important to help me achieve
Intellectual: My thoughts are important to help me achieve
Physical: My actions are important to help me achieve
Spiritual: My spirit is important to help me achieve

Once we feel reasonably safe in the world, we can let go of fear and shift energy toward accomplishing our objectives. The building years of life require us to acquire knowledge and skills to build our status in our domain of choice. With years comes wisdom in our field, and we begin to feel a sense of accomplishment. Wherever people go they can sense where they stand regarding people around them. We desire status because of the sense of accomplishment it gives us inside. Sure, the external rewards are nice, but they can never make up for low self-esteem.

This makes me think of a client who was plagued with a sense of self that didn't quite measure up. On the outside she appeared very successful, dressed in beautiful clothes, and she had risen to the highest rank possible in her division of the company where she'd worked for the last two decades. Her problem was the judgment she had placed on herself about her education. She had finished high school and not gone to college, instead completing an online university degree. She had been in the same company for years, getting promoted numerous times. The dilemma seemed to be that she wanted to consider leaving her current employer to pursue a new challenge, but the online university had been put out of business for some questionable practices. All of a sudden, her identity in regard to importance appeared to be in question in her view of herself.

I knew she had to answer the question "Am I enough?" with or without the degree. So we set out to do the work to answer this question. One option was to enroll in a university and do the work again. Another was to take the questionable degree off her resume and proceed in a job search without higher education on there. A third was to leave it there and take the responsibility of explaining the situation if it came up, which felt dicey. There were others, but these were the main three options she settled on. I knew that this debate would have to be settled by her and her alone. I could sense that she wanted me to have the answers, but of course her sense of her identity was not my territory.

She did her homework and seriously considered applying for secondary education again. To her, the other two options were ruled out early. With a full-time executive role in such a big company, with travel and a social life, it was going to be a challenge to add going to college in the mix, but I knew she had to go through the discovery to make a decision. While she did her homework, I continued to ask her about her career. As her story poured forth, I think we both began to realize that she had a solid case of evidence to help her acknowledge her relative importance in her company. And as luck would have it, she was also being recruited by a competitor who had heard of her accomplishments. Over the course of a few months, I think her view of herself changed, and she eventually decided not to get that degree and that she had done just fine without it.

Some of what helped was having someone to witness her questions and her discovery journey. But mostly it was her own effort to conduct the research and answer her own questions about her worth in her own mind. She had to estimate herself by another measure that mattered as much or even more than a piece of paper. I would have supported her no matter what she decided, but to me, it did seem unnecessary to get that piece of paper thirty-five years later, when she had already achieved so much. In the course of four short months, she held her shoulders a little higher each time she left my office. She was a courageous person and a very creative strategic thinker. But in the end, she had to check that box for herself to be satisfied. She owned her importance in her demeanor, her firm eye contact, and in her voice. It was all over her. We just had to clear up a little detail.

Practice

Keep records of your goals for life and work, and write them in journals once a year. Take the time to acknowledge the things you do that get you one step closer to that ultimate sense of accomplishment you want to feel one day. Enjoy some of it right now and celebrate along the way.

If you answered no to this question

Take some time to imagine a five-year goal that would make you feel important in your own estimation. Then work backward to break that goal into chunks that you can accomplish one year at a time, one month at a time, one day at a time. Then commit to taking that first step tomorrow.

REFLECTION:

If you had to answer this question for yourself at this juncture in your life, how close would you be to checking the box that says "I am important, in my own right, and right where I should be right now"? What can you acknowledge that you have achieved so far that is deserving of your own satisfaction? What status and significance makes you feel that your efforts in the world are important?

Our responsibility is to change what we know needs work and trust that our inner saboteur will have the courage to disrupt what we cannot yet see.

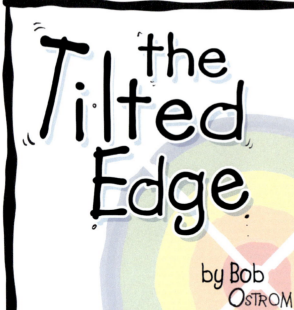

Question #6
☐ Am I productive?
(Autonomy vs. Dependence)

The underlying need is to experience taking initiative on your own behalf, establishing independence and being productive enough to take care of yourself, your family, and your future. This requires moving beyond feeling capable or competent to actually applying those skills to provide for a good life and build up reserves that satisfy your needs and standards for living.

Significant relationships: Peers, friends, partners, mentors, spouse, children

Goal: Autonomy and independence

Fear: Vulnerability

Four Outcomes

Emotional: I can manage my own feelings

Intellectual: I can learn what I need to know

Physical: I can provide physically for myself

Spiritual: I can provide hope for my own future

Once we feel reasonably capable and competent, we can let go of fear and shift energy to focus on expanding our productivity and contributions to our chosen field of work or domain. The word successful has to be defined by you, but it often means an accumulation of wealth, accomplishments, goals, respect, recognition, and contributions to your field, or other thriving that occurs once you have found your place in the world. Today people live almost twice the number of years as previous generations and thus may have the chance to experience success in more than one career endeavor. Success can also be defined by social affluence and work contribution. Whatever your definition, you get to decide for yourself.

If success is a never-ending goal that feels insatiable to you, then you may be working on unfinished ego business. This makes me think of quite a few clients I've worked with over the years, since it's such a common pattern. As an example, let's consider the story of a VP of sales I coached a few years ago. She worked in a large established company and hired me to coach her because of her "style." She had been told by her supervisor and by recent feedback from peers that she was too aggressive for the culture of the company, which she had just joined a year ago.

My own experience of her was that she moved fast, made decisions, and said what she meant, and she was getting feedback that she was just not "the right fit" at that particular company. She described the culture as nice, diplomatic, forgiving, and thoughtful, but also conflict avoidant. I re-

member her saying, "No one is held accountable. If someone doesn't do well, they just move them to another job that is less impactful, but no one is ever held accountable." To her, the culture was maddening, and it was definitely triggering some FOO stories for her. When I asked her to play devil's advocate and explore the bright side, she laughed and said, "At least I don't have to worry about getting fired. A nice bonus if you don't have big dreams for your career. But I do have big dreams for my career. Right now, I feel underutilized. Bored. Badly enough that I'm taking calls from recruiters."

As I listened to her, I knew the question of success was driving her tendency to aggressive behavior. Granted, I agreed with her that the culture leaned on the side of valuing people more than results, but I also suggested there was no perfect culture and we had to stop judging the situation as "one side is right and one side is wrong." What if she was okay to want what she wanted and the culture was okay to be the way it was? It might just be a fit problem, after all. And she wasn't going to be able to change the culture anytime soon. She could influence it, but changing it was another matter.

We decided to look at the facts and explore her stories about what was so horrible to her when people were not held accountable. Not in general, but what it meant to her—her own story about it. That was the problem. It upset her a lot. She would get aggressive and judgmental, which then reinforced to others that being diplomatic was better. I knew there were some organizational FOO stories going on there in the cultural tendencies too, but that wasn't my business. She was my client and what we had to do was help her get in touch with her own truths and definitions of success as it related to her choices and responsibility. Was she striving too hard, getting herself upset, and then showing up with a fear-based mindset? Or taking responsibility for being a free, reasonable, mature professional who had choices?

What it boiled down to was a parent mindset that came from her family. Her story was that people must be held accountable no matter what. When we dug into this, her energy shifted to her own family and she began to see how strong her striving to meet this hidden message was—how it affected her marriage, her friendships, and even her kids. Once she saw her own striving, she began to see the self-fulfilling prophecy of her story. Everywhere she went she looked for people to hold accountable and then was relentless about straightening them up or being the hero to change it.

One day in a coaching session I decided to make a point. I decided to play her, and in a very parent-like voice told her what she should do. This was a break from the norm and not how I usually showed up. Her reaction was to tear up and withdraw. I asked her to describe in detail how it had made her feel. The FOO stories came out automatically. I had been acting like her dad . . . and so had she! All her life. Why? She had mimicked his unbending strength so he would see her as successful. That day was a huge breakthrough, and she was able to see how she was making others feel. Everything changed after that. We redefined success in a new way—her new way—and her energy shifted to a whole different demeanor. The problem of feeling like a poor fit to the culture went away, and she has created even more success for herself and her colleagues by being an example of success for others. The company culture has even begun to shift and people are holding themselves more accountable!

Practice

Write down small successes along the way in your life and career. Celebrate the wins and stop to appreciate the effort and hard work it took to accomplish them. Adding points over time serves to improve your self-respect. Then you will get more respect in return, too.

If you answered no to this question

Take an inventory of your past successes, small or large. Divide your life into decades on a piece of paper and write down the significant accomplishments you made in each decade. Some will be high, some low. Also, make an inventory of things you might call a failure. Reframe them as "lessons learned" and notice what happened after the lesson. Often the worst times in our lives are the most memorable catalysts for change and an upward trend occurs afterward. Decide that next time you are tempted to label yourself as a failure, you will rewrite the story, and commit to seeing it as a pivot to try something different next time.

REFLECTION:

Take a few moments to define what success means to you and what it looks like in manifest form in your life. How does a successful person show up? Can you check this box for yourself and feel complete? Or do you have work to do? Can you commit to examining how your stories are either helping others or hindering them from their own success?

My Notes

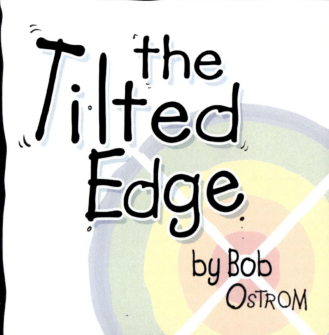

Question #7
☐ Am I valued?
(Acceptance vs. Isolation)

The underlying need is to experience being appreciated and valued enough to make your presence in this world matter. This requires moving beyond being a good person to actually demonstrating social value through contributions and service to society.

Significant relationships: Work, family, friends
Goal: Social acceptance and affirmation

Four Outcomes
Emotional: I contribute compassion to my community
Intellectual: I contribute my achievements to my community
Physical: I contribute my actions to my community
Spiritual: I contribute hope to my community

  Innate in all of us is the desire to be accepted by others and to belong to a group of like-minded people in our profession, personal circles, or both. But we are also members of society and benefactors of everyone who lives in our community with us. People can't live in total isolation, even if they tried, unless they go live in the woods and eat off the land. As human beings we depend upon one another and we thrive when all of us thrive. You can be a good person all by yourself, but unless you are interacting with others, does it actually still matter?

When you think about all of the things we take for granted, it's easy to think you don't need anybody, but you actually do. You need the people who made the streets you drive on. You need the people who grow and package the food you eat. You need someone to drill the fuels you consume. And so on. This aspect of identity requires a level of thinking that conveys an understanding of the big picture. We can't complain about the economy if we are not part of what helps it thrive. Or complain no one cares about us if we aren't willing to serve in community organizations that serve our spiritual growth. This aspect of identity is about understanding we are all part of a whole and therefore responsible for giving our services and efforts back if we participate in taking.

This reminds me of a client I worked with recently who was struggling with this part of himself. He considered himself a good guy, and I would agree. Many people would call him lucky, since his family had left him a small fortune and he was independently wealthy, well beyond others in their early twenties. But I think this luck was actually preventing him from grappling with the normal struggles people usually go through at his age, in early adulthood. He didn't have to work, but that didn't quite feel right to him either. All his friends were busy with careers, getting married, or starting families. He had a job, but it had been the third one he'd tried in the last few years, and he didn't feel engaged in any of them. He said he felt lost and was looking for his purpose. He was reading books about finding his purpose, but nothing had seemed to get him over the hump. He spent his time playing golf all day or partying with friends on weekends, and hanging out at home during the week after work, watching TV.

From the very beginning of his coaching with me, I knew the problem was within him and had to do with his identity. And the problem was that he had been robbed of the experience of having to struggle and grapple with life to make something of himself like most people his age. It was about the money that his parents left him with good intentions. I also figured that they left it to him because of their own FOO stories of hardship, from starting life poor or something like that. I am sure they had good intentions, but this decision was of devastating consequence to this man's sense of self.

As we worked together, I explained that sometimes it takes more than just being a good person to accomplish this part of our identity. We also have to make something of ourselves and contribute back to the community or world we live in. I wished I had said this earlier, because this one idea changed everything. As an example, I told him about a recent experience I'd had in an airport, where a young pregnant woman was in the security line in front of me. She didn't want to go through the

X-ray machine and security gave her a hard time about it, directing her to go over to the other side far away. She had bags and a computer and coat that had already gone through on the conveyor belt, so she was quite upset about losing contact with her belongings. I could tell the security people had not connected her being pregnant with not wanting to go along with the security procedures, so when I got to the other side, I gathered her things and explained the situation to another security official, who helped by waving to her while he put her things where she could see them.

The point I made in telling my client this story was that I walked away feeling like I had done the right thing, even though I was slightly in danger of missing my own connection. It felt right, so I did it. Not for credit, but to give of myself to someone in need. It made me feel deeply grateful inside that I could do this for her and relieve a little bit of stress for this traveling businesswoman and her child. And for whatever reason, this story is what changed everything for my client.

He was off and running as he began to tune in to what he could do for other people with his hands and his resources. He began to light up inside. Before long he was engaged in researching what he might be able to do with a much wider lens as he searched for a worthy vocation. It's still early in his life, but it was easy to conclude that his work with me was finished, because he became busy with his new venture and was on fire with energy. I guess the lesson is that sometimes life can get ahead of us. What he needed was to be able to challenge himself like everyone else. And once he got outside himself, his sullen passivity turned into passion. I fully expect him to make something of himself and believe he may change the world in some important ways with his work one day.

Practice
Take a few minutes every day to count your blessings. What can you be grateful for from others in your life? Stop and send one note of thanks. Or call one old friend or teacher. Or say thank you to someone who just served you. Or stop to notice someone in need and give them a hand. Even if you are in a hurry.

If you answered no to this question
If you don't feel valued, what's your story about this? What are you saying to yourself about others or the world? When in your life did you not feel valued? Are there any times that you are unable to forget? How can you begin to give to others in your community that which you didn't get yourself long ago? How can you show your respect for how all of us are in this together?

REFLECTION:

Make a list of all of the activities you do in a typical week and list all of the skills of others it takes to provide what you consume. Take the time to reflect and marvel at our ability to coexist together and provide for the needs of people we will likely never meet. Then think about how you are extra special in a certain way and contribute back to people you will know or not know. How does your life give back to the world? Acknowledge the skills you bring to your community and smile.

My Notes

Be mindful of the judgments you pass on yourself, for they will be revealed to the world in everything you say and do.

Question # 8
☐ Am I worthy?
(Recognition vs. Despair)

The underlying need is to experience being recognized and feeling self-worth because all of the other dilemmas are also complete. This requires moving beyond being an individual that is free, to finding your own voice, expressing it through your creative purpose, and making a unique difference in the world in some way.

Significant relationships: Those closest to you who have been a witness to your life. Those who may never know you but nevertheless benefit from your efforts.

Goal: Recognition and fulfillment

Fear: I will not be remembered

Four Outcomes

Emotional: The work of my heart will live beyond me

Intellectual: The work of my mind will live beyond me

Physical: The work of my actions will live beyond me

Spiritual: The work of my spirit will live beyond me

Leaving a legacy means you have been productive, creative, and innovative in ways that actually improved the world for good for future generations beyond your lifespan. It obviously requires the other seven questions be mostly satisfied for you to transcend into thinking about a world beyond your life. Some might say it requires selflessness, but I actually think the opposite. I think it requires you to think highly enough of yourself that you give yourself permission to spend your life on a great body of work that makes you happy beyond reason. In that way, there is an inclusion of self in the idea, because you cannot truly find your purpose without finding your passion, too. Choosing to devote extreme amounts of effort and decades of your life in service of a mission that no one cares about as much as you might be considered by some as the ultimate act of selfishness in some ways.

I truly think we become one with our greatest work when it becomes a labor of love and consumes every ounce of our energy, intellect, and creative imagination. What comes to mind is the musician who drags their tired body onto the stage and comes to life when the first note plays. Or the researcher laboring late into the night for forty years, trying to find a cure for cancer. The rich entrepreneur who spends their fortune on their crazy dream to build a rocket that will take us to Mars. Or another billionaire entrepreneur who donates 99 percent of their wealth to educate the next generation of children. Or the fundraiser for hospices who is recognized for their contributions, inducted into their city's hall of fame five years after their own death, and not forgotten by so many who appreciated their devotion. But this can also be demonstrated by less visible people. Like the retired lady across the street who spends every evening at Alcoholics Anonymous meetings and gives all of her time to sponsor deeply frightened addicts who have somehow found the courage to ask for help and take responsibility. Or the bright lawyer who serves those who cannot afford to hire a lawyer themselves. And so many more examples in all walks of life.

In fact, I can find this kind of hero in so many stories and lives I've encountered that it's the one driving force that gives me energy in the moments I need it most . . . when my own creative work feels too hard for one person to complete. This is the final question we have to answer when we find that creative imperative and say yes to it. The idea is easy. It's the years of hard work to accomplish something of substance for the next generation that helps us know we, ourselves, are complete. When the rewards will be felt by people we will never know. That is what builds rock-solid presence. You earn it and there it is.

REFLECTION:

Now, go back to your Tilt Presence Wheel and reflect on how you're doing with the last four questions. This reflection exercise will tell you what is next in your development and the actualization of your unique creative purpose. There are no age categories because these can actualize at any adult age. Ultimately, you would want to answer them all fully to feel complete and fulfilled in every aspect of life. The longer you live, the more fully the tasks can be rounded out and polished for further experience of fulfillment and personal happiness.

 Note that these four categories are more complex and sophisticated than the first four, which are more basic in helping you move into adulthood. Notice that the more complete your wheel, the more you become your most authentic, true self. You don't need more from others than they are willing to give. The hole inside has become full, and the fruit from your life brims over with gratitude and integrity to your true self. Your voice has been heard, your contributions have been of value, you have provided for those you love, and you are supported by a community of those who love you.

FINAL REFLECTION:

The surprising paradox of all is found in this exercise which brings your life and work into explicit clarity. What is most profound in the end is that when the identity settles into reality, an opposite awareness is experienced. You will know you are complete when these four truths arise:

- Instead of seeking status, you find peace in the truth that you are ultimately insignificant.
- Instead of seeking power, you find peace in the truth that you are ultimately vulnerable.
- Instead of seeking approval, you find peace in the truth that you are ultimately alone.
- Instead of seeking attention, you find peace in the truth that you are ultimately ordinary.

This may seem strange and untenable to you if you are in your learning and building up years. But that is where you will find ultimate peace and joy in your giving back years. It is the final letting go of ego that is able to see reality in such stark light and find the silver lining of joy.

So...

"Whatever you can do, or dream you can do, begin it.
Boldness has genius, power, and magic in it.
Begin it now."

INVITATION TO THE TILT APPROACH

If the concepts in this book interest you and you want to learn more about what drives your personality, behavior and character, we have developed a self-assessment that can shed light on which of the four primary existential questions may be driving unconscious patterns that are shaping your outcomes. The best place to start is with the True Tilt Profile self-assessment that takes only ten minutes to complete and will get you on the right path to self-knowledge. Go to www.tilt365.com and get started today.

"Until you make the unconscious conscious, it will direct your life and you will call it fate."
—C.G. Jung

Credits to bodies of work that have informed the topics in this book:

Aristotle
Eric Berne
Nathaniel Brandon
Carol Dweck
Erik Erikson
Katie Hendricks
Carl Jung
Carol Pearson
Ken Wilbur
VIA Institute

PAM BONEY: A thought leader in the domain of character science, Pam Boney is a futurist and innovator in the human analytics domain. Pam is the Founder and CEO of Tilt365, designing talent development assessments and team culture diagnostics and solutions for leaders and teams, to catalyze exponential change by building character strengths and creating cultural agility. Author of several books and featured regularly in industry leading publications and blogs, her passion is to shore up the greatest blind spot of our time —character intelligence. With it, we disrupt ego-politics and divert more energy into productivity, creativity and innovation. Without it, we may never be able to innovate fast enough to solve the most important and complex problems of a global world.

BOB OSTROM: Bob is an illustrator who got his start designing cartoon characters over 25 years ago. Since then Bob's work has been featured in over 250 books and publications for companies like Disney, Cartoon Network, Nickelodeon and many, many more.

Two years ago Bob teamed up with Pam Boney as a Creative Director to design a special line of characters for Tilt 365. **The Tilted Edge** comic strip, featuring 4 lizard characters each representing a different part of the lizard brain, can now be found at Tilt365.com.

PLEASE LEAVE US A REVIEW:

If you find this book helpful we would really appreciate a product review to share with other potential readers.

Made in the USA
Columbia, SC
31 May 2019